GOOD HOUSEKEEPING

CHINESE COOKING

Here are delicious recipes gathered from every corner of China. Some fragrantly fresh with ginger and sesame, others sizzlingly spicy with garlic and chillies. The simple step-by-step recipes guide you through the techniques of Chinese cookery to help you produce authentic meals which will impress your family and friends. For a really Eastern touch, discard your cutlery and bring on the chopsticks....

With the compliments of

COOKERY NOTES

Follow either metric or imperial measures for the recipes in this book as they are not inter-changeable. Sets of spoon measures are available in both metric and imperial size to give accurate measurement of small quantities. All spoon measures are level unless otherwise stated. When measuring milk we have used the exact conversion of 568 ml (1 pint).
* Size 2 eggs should be used except when otherwise stated.
† Granulated sugar is used un-less otherwise stated.
● Plain flour is used unless otherwise stated.

OVEN TEMPERATURE CHART

°C	°F	Gas mark
110	225	$\frac{1}{4}$
130	250	$\frac{1}{2}$
140	275	1
150	300	2
170	325	3
180	350	4
190	375	5
200	400	6
220	425	7
230	450	8
240	475	9

KEY TO SYMBOLS

$\boxed{1.00*}$ Indicates minimum preparation and cooking times in hours and minutes. They do not include prepared items in the list of ingredients; calculated times apply only to the method. An asterisk * indicates extra time should be allowed, so check the note below symbols.

⌂ Chef's hats indicate degree of difficulty of a recipe: no hat means it is straightforward; one hat slightly more complicated; two hats indicates that it is for more advanced cooks.

£ Indicates a recipe which is good value for money; £ £ indicates an expensive recipe. No £ sign indicates an inexpensive recipe.

✳ Indicates that a recipe will freeze. If there is no symbol, the recipe is unsuitable for freezing. An asterisk * indicates special freezer instructions so check the note immediately below the symbols.

$\boxed{309 \text{ cals}}$ Indicates calories per serving, including any sugges-tions (e.g. cream, to serve) given in the ingredients.

METRIC CONVERSION SCALE

LIQUID			SOLID		
Imperial	Exact conversion	Recommended ml	Imperial	Exact conversion	Recommended g
$\frac{1}{4}$ pint	142 ml	150 ml	1 oz	28.35 g	25 g
$\frac{1}{2}$ pint	284 ml	300 ml	2 oz	56.7 g	50 g
1 pint	568 ml	600 ml	4 oz	113.4 g	100 g
$1\frac{1}{2}$ pints	851 ml	900 ml	8 oz	226.8 g	225 g
$1\frac{3}{4}$ pints	992 ml	1 litre	12 oz	340.2 g	350 g
For quantities of $1\frac{3}{4}$ pints and over, litres and fractions of a litre have been used.			14 oz	397.0 g	400 g
			16 oz (1 lb)	453.6 g	450 g
			1 kilogram (kg) equals 2.2 lb.		

Illustrated on the cover: Stir-fried Pork and Vegetables (page 25)

GOOD HOUSEKEEPING

CHINESE COOKING

Contents

CHINESE EGG SOUP

0.15* | 210 cals

* plus 20 minutes soaking mushrooms

Serves 2

2 Chinese dried mushrooms, soaked

50 g (2 oz) cooked leftover meat (e.g. pork, chicken, beef or lamb)

450 ml ($\frac{3}{4}$ pint) chicken stock

100 g (4 oz) tofu (see box)

30 ml (2 tbsp) cider vinegar

30 ml (2 tbsp) soy sauce

2 eggs

5 ml (1 tsp) chilli oil, or to taste (see box)

salt

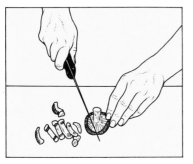

1 Drain the mushrooms, then slice very thinly. Slice the leftover meat very thinly.

2 Pour the stock into a saucepan and bring to the boil. Add the mushrooms and meat and simmer for 5 minutes.

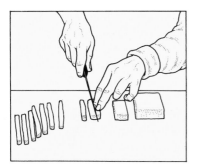

3 Meanwhile, drain the tofu and pat dry. Cut into thin strips. Add to the pan with the vinegar and soy sauce. Heat gently.

4 Crack the eggs into a bowl and add chilli oil, to taste. Beat well. Pour into the hot soup in a thin, steady stream, then stir vigorously with a fork until the eggs form threads. Taste and add salt, then pour into warmed soup bowls. Serve immediately.

CHINESE EGG SOUP

Tofu, also called bean curd because it is made from soya beans, is used extensively in oriental cooking for its nutritional value—it has a very high protein content. There are two types available from health food shops and oriental stores. Silken tofu, the Japanese variety, is soft, whereas the Chinese bean curd (called *doufu*) is firm and sold in cakes or blocks. Both varieties are suitable for this soup.

Hot chilli oil can be bought in bottles from oriental stores, but it can also be made quickly and easily at home. Fry chopped dried red chillies in hot corn oil, leave to steep for 2 days, then strain into a jar with a screw-topped lid. Stored in the refrigerator, it will keep indefinitely.

HOT AND SOUR SOUP

| 0.30 | ⊟ £ £ ✳ | 136 cals |

Serves 4

225 g (8 oz) button mushrooms

100 ml (4 fl oz) medium dry sherry

75 ml (5 tbsp) soy sauce

30 ml (2 tbsp) chopped fresh
   coriander

225 g (8 oz) cooked chicken or pork

125 g (4 oz) spring onions

125 g (4.4 oz) jar whole baby
   sweetcorn

75 ml (5 tbsp) white wine vinegar

freshly ground pepper

1 Slice the mushrooms thinly.
   Place in a large saucepan with
the sherry, soy sauce, coriander
and 1.1 litres (2 pints) water. Bring
to the boil. Simmer, uncovered,
for 15 minutes.

2 Thinly shred the chicken (or
   finely dice the pork) and
spring onions. Thinly slice the
sweetcorn.

3 Stir the prepared meat and
   vegetables into the mushroom
mixture, with the wine vinegar
and season to taste with pepper.
Simmer for a further 5 minutes.
Serve hot.

CHINESE CHICKEN SOUP

| 1.00 | £ £ | ✳ | 260 cals |

Serves 4

25 g (1 oz) dried mushrooms

100 g (4 oz) boneless chicken breast, skinned

1 bunch of spring onions, trimmed

1.1 litres (2 pints) chicken stock

60 ml (4 tbsp) dry or medium sherry

30 ml (2 tbsp) soy sauce, or to taste

5-cm (2-inch) piece of fresh root ginger, peeled and crushed

50 g (2 oz) lean boiled ham

227-g (8-oz) can sliced bamboo shoots, drained

100 g (4 oz) Chinese noodles

salt and freshly ground pepper

prawn crackers, to serve

1 Soak the dried mushrooms in a bowl of warm water for 30 minutes.

2 Meanwhile, cut the chicken into thin matchstick strips and slice the spring onions diagonally into 2.5-cm (1-inch) lengths.

3 Bring the stock to the boil in a large saucepan. Add the sherry, 30 ml (2 tbsp) soy sauce and the ginger, lower the heat then add the chicken, spring onions and drained and sliced mushrooms. Cover and cook for 10 minutes until the chicken is tender.

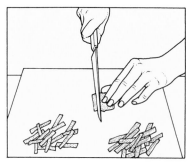

4 Cut the ham and bamboo shoots into thin matchstick strips. Add to the soup with the noodles and simmer for about 5 minutes until the noodles are tender. Add salt and pepper to taste, with more soy sauce if liked. Pour into warmed individual soup bowls and serve immediately, accompanied by prawn crackers.

CHINESE CHICKEN SOUP

Dried mushrooms, bamboo shoots, fresh ginger and Chinese noodles can all be found in Chinese supermarkets or specialist food shops. Ginger root is also sold in many West Indian and Asian stores. Don't be tempted to substitute fresh mushrooms for dried—the flavour of dried mushrooms is much stronger and helps to give the soup its characteristic body and taste. They are used extensively in Chinese cookery.

SESAME PRAWN TOASTS

0.45* £ £ 323 cals

* plus 30 minutes chilling

Serves 6

700 g (1½ lb) raw Pacific prawns, or frozen scampi, thawed

1 cm (½ inch) piece fresh root ginger, peeled and finely chopped

7.5 ml (1½ tsp) cornflour

10 ml (2 tsp) dry sherry

1 egg white, beaten

5 ml (1 tsp) salt

a pinch of sugar

6–8 slices white bread, left out for about 2 hours

75 g (3 oz) sesame seeds

6 water chestnuts, finely chopped (optional)

vegetable oil, for frying

spring onions, to garnish

chilli sauce, to serve

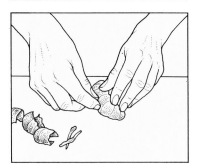

1 If using Pacific prawns, remove the legs and with a sharp knife, make a slit down the centre of the back and remove the intestinal vein. Wash well. If using scampi, rinse and pat dry with absorbent kitchen paper.

2 Put the prawns into a food processor with the ginger and work to a smooth paste.

3 Mix the cornflour, sherry and egg white in a jug with the salt and sugar. Add gradually to the prawn paste. Do not overwork or the mixture will become too light when cooked. Cover and chill in the refrigerator for 30 minutes.

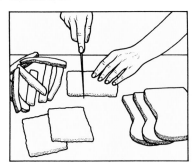

4 Meanwhile, cut the crusts off the bread and make into squares.

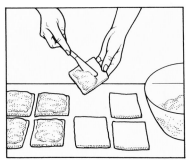

5 If using water chestnuts, add them to the prawn mixture and stir well. Spread a generous amount of paste on 1 side of each slice of bread, about 0.5 cm–1 cm (¼–½ inch) thick, less at the edges.

6 Dip the prawn side of the bread into the sesame seeds and press lightly to coat.

7 Heat the oil in a deep-fat frier to 180°C (350°F). Slide 2 prawn toasts at a time into the hot oil. Deep fry for 3 minutes, turning once, until golden brown. Remove with a slotted spoon and drain. Keep warm in a low oven.

8 Cut each prawn toast diagonally into 4 small triangles. Arrange on a serving dish and garnish with spring onion brushes. Serve with chilli sauce.

PANCAKE ROLLS

| 0.40 | 🗍🗍 £ ✳* | 99 cals |

* freeze after step 7

Makes 8

225 g (8 oz) cooked chicken

15 ml (1 tbsp) sesame or vegetable oil

1 small bunch of spring onions, trimmed and finely chopped

3 garlic cloves, skinned and crushed

2.5-cm (1-inch) piece of fresh root ginger, peeled and crushed

100 g (4 oz) beansprouts

2 carrots, peeled and grated

15 ml (1 tbsp) soy sauce

2.5 ml ($\frac{1}{2}$ tsp) soft brown sugar

salt and freshly ground pepper

8 squares of spring roll pastry, defrosted if frozen

vegetable oil, for deep-frying

1 Cut the chicken into thin strips, discarding any pieces of skin or bone. Set aside.

2 Heat the 15 ml (1 tbsp) oil in a wok or frying pan, add the spring onions, garlic and ginger and fry gently for 5 minutes until soft. Add the beansprouts and carrot and fry for a further 2 minutes, stirring constantly.

3 Turn the vegetables into a bowl, add the chicken, and mix with the soy sauce, sugar and salt and pepper to taste.

4 Divide the filling mixture equally into eight, then form each portion into a roll shape.

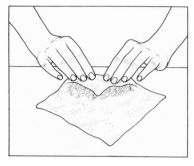

5 Place one roll on one sheet of pastry, over the corner nearest to you. Fold over the corner.

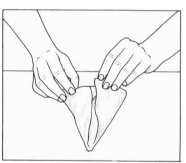

6 Fold in the corner at right angles to the first corner, then fold in the opposite corner.

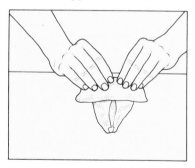

7 Roll up the filling in the pastry until the last corner is reached, so that the filling is completely enclosed. Seal with a little water.

8 Heat the oil to 180°C (350°F), then deep-fry the rolls for about 5 minutes. Drain well.

ORIENTAL SEAFOOD SALAD

0.15	£ £	405 cals

Serves 4

30 ml (2 tbsp) sesame oil

½ small onion, peeled and very finely chopped

2.5-cm (1-inch) piece fresh root ginger, peeled and crushed

10 ml (2 tsp) soy sauce, or to taste

120 ml (8 tbsp) mayonnaise

salt and freshly ground pepper

225 g (8 oz) peeled prawns

225 g (8 oz) white crabmeat, flaked

1 red pepper, cored, seeded and diced

¼ cucumber, diced

50 g (2 oz) fresh beansprouts

few Chinese leaves or lettuce leaves

juice of 1 lime

lime slices and unpeeled prawns, to garnish

1 Heat the oil in a small pan, add the onion and ginger and fry gently until soft. Remove from the heat, transfer to a large bowl and leave to cool.

2 Stir in the soy sauce and mayonnaise, with salt and freshly ground pepper to taste.

3 Fold prawns and crabmeat gently into mayonnaise mixture, then fold in red pepper, cucumber and beansprouts. Adjust seasoning, remembering that soy sauce is itself quite salty.

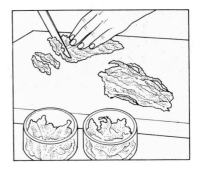

3 Meanwhile, shred the Chinese leaves or lettuce and use to line four glass dishes. To serve, pile the cocktail in the centre, then squeeze a little lime juice over each serving. Serve garnished with lime slices and unpeeled prawns.

QUICK BEEF STIR FRY

0.40*	504 cals

* plus overnight marinating

Serves 4

450 g (1 lb) shin of beef, trimmed
   of fat and sinew

45 ml (3 tbsp) medium sherry

30 ml (2 tbsp) lemon juice

15 ml (1 tbsp) soy sauce

10 ml (2 tsp) paprika

2 medium onions, skinned

125 g (4 oz) button mushrooms

225 g (8 oz) long grain rice

salt and freshly ground pepper

about 45 ml (3 tbsp) peanut or
   vegetable oil

2 Put the sherry in a bowl with the lemon juice, soy sauce and paprika. Whisk together, then add the strips of beef. Stir well, cover and leave to marinate in the refrigerator overnight.

3 The next day, slice the onions and mushrooms thinly. Cook the rice in plenty of boiling salted water for about 12 minutes until just tender. Drain well.

4 Remove the meat from the marinade with a slotted spoon. Heat 45 ml (3 tbsp) oil in a wok or large frying pan until smoky hot.

6 Stir in the sliced onions and mushrooms, adding more oil if necessary. Stir fry for a further 2 minutes, then add the rice and marinade mixture.

7 Reduce the heat and stir fry until the meat is tender and the ingredients are thoroughly combined and heated through. Add salt and pepper to taste. Serve immediately.

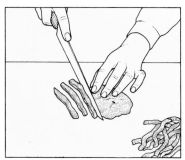

1 Slice the meat wafer thin and shred into matchstick-long strips with a very sharp knife.

5 Add the meat to the wok and stir fry over high heat for about 2 minutes.

SZECHUAN SHREDDED BEEF

1.00	☐ £ £	274 cals

Serves 4

350 g (12 oz) beef skirt or rump
  steak

2 fresh red or green chillies

1 large onion

2 garlic cloves

5 cm (1 inch) piece of fresh root
  ginger

225 g (8 oz) can bamboo shoots,
  drained

2 medium red peppers

75 ml (5 tbsp) hoisin sauce

60 ml (4 tbsp) dry sherry

30 ml (2 tbsp) corn or vegetable oil

15 ml (1 tbsp) sesame oil

1 Put the steak in the freezer for at least 20 minutes, to make it easier to slice thinly.

2 Meanwhile, prepare the vegetables. Trim the ends off the chillies and slice each one in half lengthways. Hold the chillies under cold running water and remove the seeds. Rinse your hands and pat the chillies dry with absorbent kitchen paper.

3 Chop the chillies finely. Skin the onion and slice thinly. Skin the garlic and crush to a paste.

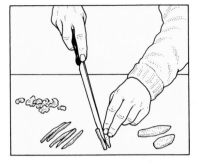

4 Peel the fresh ginger and slice the flesh into thin matchstick strips. Slice the bamboo shoots thinly.

5 Cut the stalk ends off the red peppers and cut out and discard the cores and seeds. Wash the peppers and pat dry with absorbent kitchen paper.

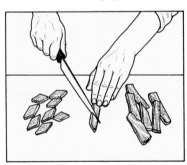

6 Cut the peppers into strips about 5 mm (¼ inch) wide. Cut each strip across diagonally to make 'diamond' shapes.

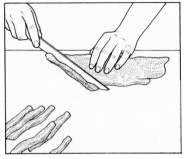

7 Cut the steak into thin slices, then stack several slices one on top of another. With a meat cleaver or very sharp knife, cut lengthways into thin matchstick strips. Put the strips of steak in a bowl, add the hoisin sauce and sherry and stir. Leave to marinate while cooking the vegetables.

8 Heat the oil in a wok until smoking hot. Add the chillies, onion and garlic and stir fry over moderate heat for 3–4 minutes until softened. Remove with a slotted spoon and set aside. Add the red peppers, increase the heat and stir fry for a few seconds. Remove with a slotted spoon and set aside with the chillies.

9 Add the steak and marinade to the wok in batches. Stir fry each batch over high heat for about 2 minutes, removing each batch with a slotted spoon.

10 Return the vegetables to the wok. Add the ginger and bamboo shoots, then the meat and stir fry for a further minute to heat through.

11 Turn the mixture into a warmed serving dish, sprinkle with the sesame oil and serve immediately.

CHINESE BEEF WITH MUSHROOMS AND OYSTER SAUCE

| 0.40 | £ £ | 408 cals |

Serves 2

25 g (1 oz) Chinese dried
  mushrooms

175–225 g (6–8 oz) rump steak

30 ml (2 tbsp) oyster sauce
  (see box)

30 ml (2 tbsp) dry sherry

salt and freshly ground pepper

30 ml (2 tbsp) vegetable oil

1 small onion, skinned and thinly
  sliced

1 garlic clove, skinned and crushed

2.5 cm (1 inch) piece of fresh root
  ginger, peeled

2 carrots, peeled

10 ml (2 tsp) cornflour

1 Put the dried mushrooms in a
bowl, pour in boiling water to
cover and leave to soak for about
20 minutes.

2 Meanwhile, cut the steak into
thin strips, place in a bowl and
add the oyster sauce, sherry and
salt and pepper to taste. Stir well
to mix, then cover and leave to
marinate in a cool place while the
mushrooms are soaking.

3 Heat the oil in a wok or deep,
heavy-based frying pan. Add
the onion and garlic and fry gently
for about 5 minutes until soft but
not coloured, stirring occasionally.

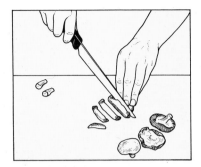

4 Meanwhile, drain the
mushrooms and reserve the
soaking liquid. Squeeze the
mushrooms dry, then slice thinly,
discarding any hard stalks. Cut
into thin matchstick strips.

5 Add the mushrooms, ginger
and carrots to the wok and stir
fry over moderate heat for about
5 minutes until slightly softened.
Add the meat and marinade and
stir fry for a few minutes more,
until the beef is tender.

6 Mix the cornflour to a paste
with 60 ml (4 tbsp) of the
soaking water from the
mushrooms. Pour into the wok
and stir fry until the sauce is
thickened. Taste and adjust
seasoning before serving.

CHINESE BEEF WITH MUSHROOMS AND OYSTER SAUCE

Look for packets of Chinese
dried mushrooms in oriental
specialist shops; they are very
expensive, but are only used in
small quantities because their
flavour is so strong. After
opening the packet, store them
carefully in an airtight jar in a
cool, dark place, where they will
keep for many months. Chinese
dried mushrooms must always be
softened in warm water for 20
minutes or so before use, so be
sure not to omit this important
part of their preparation.

Oyster sauce, as its name
suggests, is made from oysters
mixed with soy sauce and brine.
Sold in bottles in oriental shops,
it is very thick and rich, and
should be used sparingly. Once
opened, store in the refrigerator.

ORIENTAL LAMB

| 1.00 | £ | 493 cals |

Serves 4

1.4 kg (3 lb) lean shoulder of lamb
450 g (1 lb) small new potatoes
225 g (8 oz) small pickling onions
30 ml (2 tbsp) vegetable oil
25 g (1 oz) butter or margarine
15 ml (1 tbsp) flour
5 ml (1 tsp) ground ginger
300 ml ($\frac{1}{2}$ pint) chicken stock
15 ml (1 tbsp) Worcestershire sauce
30 ml (2 tbsp) soy sauce
salt and freshly ground pepper
2 caps canned pimento, diced

1 Slice all the meat off the bone, discarding any excess fat, and cut into 2.5 cm (1 inch) pieces about 5 mm ($\frac{1}{4}$ inch) thick.

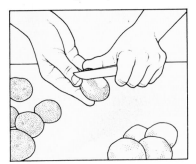

2 Wash the new potatoes and scrub them with a vegetable brush, or scrape with a knife.

3 Skin the onions. Put them in a bowl and pour in enough boiling water to cover. Leave to stand for 2 minutes, then drain and plunge into a bowl of cold water. Peel off the skin with your fingers.

4 Heat the oil and fat in a large sauté pan and brown the meat in it a few pieces at a time. Remove from the pan with a slotted spoon.

5 Add the potatoes and onions to the residual fat in the pan and fry them until lightly browned, turning frequently.

6 Return the meat to the pan, sprinkle in the flour and ginger and stir well. Cook gently, stirring, for 2 minutes.

7 Add the stock, Worcestershire sauce, soy sauce and seasoning to taste. Bring to the boil, stirring, then cover and simmer for 30 minutes or until the meat is tender.

8 Add the pimentos and stir over low heat to bring to serving temperature. Taste and adjust seasoning, then transfer to a warmed serving dish. Serve hot.

BARBECUED SPARERIBS

| 2.00 | £ | 392 cals |

Serves 4

about 1.8 kg (4 lb) Chinese-style
  pork spareribs

salt and freshly ground pepper

100 ml (4 fl oz) clear honey

60 ml (4 tbsp) dark soft brown
  sugar

60 ml (4 tbsp) tomato ketchup

30 ml (2 tbsp) Worcestershire sauce

30 ml (2 tbsp) French mustard

30 ml (2 tbsp) wine vinegar

1 If the butcher has not already
done so, cut the sheets of
spareribs into individual chops.

2 Place the ribs in 2 oiled
roasting tins and sprinkle with
salt and pepper. Roast the ribs in
the oven at 220°C (425°F) mark 7
for 20 minutes.

3 Meanwhile, put the remaining
ingredients in a jug and stir
well until mixed together.

4 Remove the ribs from the oven
and lower the temperature to
200°C (400°F) mark 6. Pour the
sauce into the tins and turn the
ribs until coated. Return to the
oven and roast for 1 hour. Turn
the ribs in the sauce several times
during cooking and swap over the
shelf positions of the 2 tins, if
necessary.

5 Lower the oven temperature
to 180°C (350°F) mark 4.
Turn the ribs over in the sauce
once more and continue roasting
for a further 30 minutes, or until
the meat is tender and the sauce
syrupy. Serve hot, with the sauce
poured over the ribs.

BARBECUED SPARERIBS

Many supermarkets now sell
Chinese-style spareribs which
are ready-cooked and only have
to be reheated for serving. These
ribs are tasty but very expensive,
and yet raw from the butcher,
spareribs are one of the most
economical cuts of meat you can
buy. Not all butchers display
spareribs because they are so
bulky, but they are well worth

asking for. Do not confuse them
with sparerib chops, which are
thicker and meatier and from the
neck end of the animal. Chinese-
style spareribs are cut from the
thick end of the belly and are
sold in sheets. The butcher will
divide them into individual ribs
if requested, which makes them
easier to deal with.

CHINESE RED-COOKED PORK

2.30 £ 887–1330 cals

Serves 4–6

1.8 kg (4 lb) rolled neck end of pork with skin

450 ml (¾ pint) chicken stock or water

200 ml (⅓ pint) soy sauce

4 garlic cloves, skinned and sliced

5 cm (2 inch) piece of fresh root ginger, peeled and sliced

10 ml (2 tsp) Chinese five-spice powder (see box)

60 ml (4 tbsp) sugar

150 ml (¼ pint) dry sherry

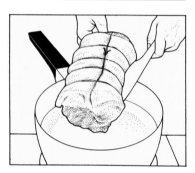

1 Bring a large saucepan of water to the boil. Add the pork and remove immediately, to scald it. Drain and pat dry.

2 Pour the stock into a large flameproof casserole. Add the soy sauce, garlic, ginger, five-spice powder and sugar. Bring to the boil, then lower the heat and simmer for 5 minutes.

3 Add the pork, skin side down, to the casserole and baste well. Cover and cook in the oven at 180°C (350°F) mark 4 for 1½ hours.

4 Remove the lid of the casserole, turn the meat skin side up and baste well with the juices. Return to the oven, uncovered, for another 30 minutes or until the pork is very tender, basting regularly.

5 Transfer the casserole to the top of the cooker. Add the dry sherry and then bring the juices to the boil.

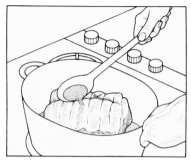

6 Boil rapidly for about 15 minutes, continually basting the meat until glazed. Take care that the meat does not catch or burn. Serve the meat sliced, hot or cold, with any remaining sauce.

SWEET AND SOUR PORK

0.30 £ 447 cals

Serves 4

700 g (1½ lb) boneless leg or shoulder of pork

20 ml (4 tsp) cornflour

salt and freshly ground pepper

vegetable oil for deep-frying, plus 15 ml (1 tbsp)

1 green pepper, cored, seeded and thinly sliced

30 ml (2 tbsp) sugar

30 ml (2 tbsp) white wine vinegar

30 ml (2 tbsp) tomato purée

30 ml (2 tbsp) pineapple juice

30 ml (2 tbsp) soy sauce

2 fresh or canned pineapple rings, finely chopped

1 Trim the fat off the pork, then cut the meat into 2.5 cm (1 inch) cubes. Coat in the corn-flour, reserving 5 ml (1 tsp) for the sauce. Add salt to taste.

2 Heat the vegetable oil in a deep-fat fryer to 180°C (350°F). Add half of the pork and deep-fry for 8–9 minutes or until tender. Remove with a slotted spoon and drain on absorbent kitchen paper. Keep hot while frying the remaining pork.

4 Add the pork and stir-fry for 1 minute. Taste and adjust seasoning, then turn into a warmed serving bowl. Serve hot.

3 Make the sauce. Heat the 15 ml (1 tbsp) vegetable oil in a wok or frying pan, add the green pepper and stir-fry for 1 minute. Stir in the remaining ingredients with the reserved cornflour. Stir-fry for 1–2 minutes.

CHINESE RED-COOKED PORK

Five-spice powder is so called because it is a mixture of five different spices. Cinnamon, cloves, fennel, star anise and Szechuan peppercorns is the usual combination, but the blend can vary from one brand to another, so that not all five-spice powder tastes the same. Look for it in packets and small jars in Chinese specialist shops, and in some large supermarkets and delicatessens. It is not absolutely essential for this dish if you are unable to obtain it, ground mixed spice can be used instead.

STIR-FRIED PORK AND VEGETABLES

0.50	433 cals

Serves 4

700 g (1½ lb) pork fillet or
    tenderloin, trimmed of fat

60 ml (4 tbsp) dry sherry

45 ml (3 tbsp) soy sauce

10 ml (2 tsp) ground ginger

salt and freshly ground pepper

1 medium cucumber

30 ml (2 tbsp) vegetable oil

1 bunch of spring onions, trimmed
    and finely chopped

1–2 garlic cloves, skinned and
    crushed (optional)

30 ml (2 tbsp) cornflour

300 ml (½ pint) chicken stock

175 g (6 oz) beansprouts

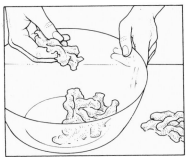

1 Cut the pork in thin strips and place in a bowl. Add the sherry, soy sauce, ginger and salt and pepper to taste, then stir well to mix. Set aside.

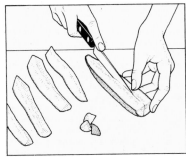

2 Prepare the cucumber sticks. Cut the cucumber in half, then cut into quarters lengthways, discarding the rounded ends. Leave the skin on, to add colour.

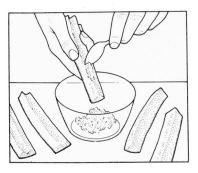

3 Using a sharp-edged teaspoon, scoop out the seeds and discard. Cut the cucumber quarters lengthways again, then slice across into strips about 2.5 cm (1 inch) long.

4 Heat the oil in a wok or large, heavy-based frying pan, add the spring onions and garlic, if using, and fry gently for about 5 minutes until softened.

5 Add the pork to the pan, increase the heat and stir-fry for 2–3 minutes until lightly coloured, tossing constantly so that it cooks evenly.

6 Mix the cornflour with the cold chicken stock and set aside.

7 Add the cucumber, spring onions and beansprouts to the pork, with the cornflour and stock. Stir-fry until the juices thicken and the ingredients are well combined. Taste and adjust seasoning, then turn into a warmed serving dish. Serve immediately.

CHILLI PORK

1.00*	£ £ ✳*	879 cals

* plus at least 4 hours marinating;
freeze after step 4

Serves 4

900 g (2 lb) pork fillets (tenderloin)

45 ml (3 tbsp) soy sauce

15 ml (1 tbsp) hoisin sauce

15 ml (1 tbsp) soft brown sugar

30 ml (2 tbsp) crushed fresh root
ginger or 10 ml (2 tsp) ground

60 ml (4 tbsp) vegetable oil

15 ml (1 tbsp) crushed dried red
chillies, or less, according to
taste

150 ml (¼ pint) chicken stock or
water

10 ml (2 tsp) cornflour

350 g (12 oz) long-grain rice,
boiled, to serve

few sliced red chillies, to garnish

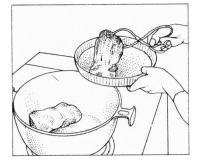

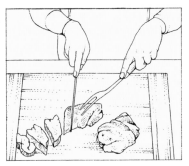

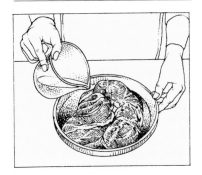

1 Place the pork fillets in a
shallow dish. Mix together the
next four ingredients with half of
the oil and pour over the pork.
Cover and leave to marinate for at
least 4 hours.

2 Heat the remaining oil in a
flameproof casserole, add
crushed chillies to taste and fry
gently for 5 minutes, stirring
all the time.

3 Remove the pork fillets from
the marinade and add to the
casserole. Fry over moderate heat,
turning constantly until browned
on all sides.

4 Mix the marinade with the
stock or water, then pour over
the pork. Bring slowly to boiling
point, then lower the heat, cover
and simmer for 45 minutes or
until the pork is tender. Baste the
pork frequently during the cooking time.

5 To serve, remove the pork
from the cooking liquid and
place on a board. Mix the cornflour to a paste with a little water,
then stir into the cooking liquid
and bring to the boil. Simmer,
stirring, until the sauce thickens.

6 Carve the pork neatly into thin
diagonal slices. Spread the hot
boiled rice out on a warmed
serving platter, arrange the pork
slices on top and spoon over some
of the sauce. Garnish with sliced
chillies and serve, with the remaining sauce handed separately.

CHILLI PORK

This recipe for Chilli Pork is
similar to the Chinese 'Red-
Cooked Pork' and the Burmese
'Red Pork' or 'Wet-thani'. Such
dishes are immensely popular in
Eastern and Oriental cookery,
where chillies are used both as a
flavouring and colouring. Dried
red chillies are easy to obtain in
Oriental and Asian stores, but if
you are unable to buy them, then
you can use chilli powder
instead. For this recipe, use 5 ml
(1 tsp) chilli powder, as the
flavour should be hot and strong,
although different brands of
chilli powder vary in their
strength, so it is best to taste
before serving in case more
needs to be added. Hoisin sauce,
also called hosin sauce and sometimes Chinese barbecue sauce, is
sold in Chinese supermarkets.
Available in cans and jars, it
keeps for months in the refrigerator once opened, and can
be used in numerous Chinese
dishes. Made from soya beans,
flour, sugar and spices, it helps
give this dish its characteristic
red colour.

CHINESE PORK AND GINGER CASSEROLE

| 1.25 | ✳* | 448 cals |

* freeze after step 4

Serves 4

30 ml (2 tbsp) vegetable oil

1 small onion, skinned and finely chopped

2.5 cm (1 inch) piece fresh root ginger

700 g (1½ lb) boneless lean pork (e.g. shoulder or sparerib), cubed

30 ml (2 tbsp) dry sherry

15 ml (1 tbsp) soy sauce

300 ml (½ pint) dry or American ginger ale

2.5 ml (½ tsp) five-spice powder

salt and freshly ground pepper

50 g (2 oz) stem ginger, sliced

½ red pepper, cored, seeded and sliced

½ yellow pepper, cored, seeded and sliced

1 Heat the oil in a flameproof casserole, add the onion and fry gently for 5 minutes until soft but not coloured.

2 Meanwhile, skin the root ginger and then crush the flesh with a mortar and pestle.

3 Add the crushed ginger to the casserole with the pork, increase the heat and fry until the meat is browned on all sides.

4 Stir in the sherry and soy sauce, then the ginger ale, five-spice powder and seasoning to taste. Bring slowly to boiling point, stirring, then lower the heat, cover and simmer for about 1 hour until the pork is just tender.

5 Add the stem ginger and pepper slices to the casserole and continue cooking for a further 10 minutes. Serve hot.

PAN-FRIED LIVER AND TOMATO

0.15* | 290 cals

* plus several hours marinating
Serves 4

450 g (1 lb) lamb's liver, sliced

30 ml (2 tbsp) Marsala or sweet
, sherry

salt and freshly ground pepper

225 g (8 oz) tomatoes, skinned

30 ml (2 tbsp) vegetable oil

2 medium onions, skinned and
finely sliced

pinch of ground ginger

150 ml ($\frac{1}{4}$ pint) chicken stock

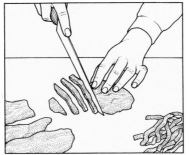

1 Using a very sharp knife, cut the liver into wafer-thin strips. Place in a shallow bowl with the Marsala or sweet sherry. Sprinkle with freshly ground pepper to taste. Cover and leave to marinate for several hours.

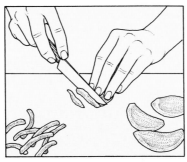

2 Cut the tomatoes into quarters and remove the seeds, reserving the juices. Slice the flesh into fine strips and set aside.

3 Heat the oil in a sauté pan or non-stick frying pan. When very hot, add the liver strips, a few at a time. Shake the pan briskly for about 30 seconds until pearls of blood appear.

4 Turn the slices and cook for a further 30 seconds only (liver hardens if it is overcooked). Remove from the pan with a slotted spoon and keep warm while cooking the remaining batches.

5 Add the onions and ginger to the residual oil in the pan and cook, uncovered, for about 5 minutes. Add the stock and seasoning to taste, return the liver to the pan and add the tomatoes and their juice. Bring just to the boil, then turn into a warmed serving dish and serve immediately.

STIR-FRIED CHICKEN WITH VEGETABLES AND CASHEW NUTS

| 0.40 | 335 cals |

Serves 4

| 1 bunch spring onions |
| 3 celery sticks |
| 1 green pepper |
| 100 g (4 oz) cauliflower florets |
| 2 carrots |
| 175 g (6 oz) button mushrooms |
| 4 boneless chicken breasts |
| 30 ml (2 tbsp) sesame or vegetable oil |
| 10 ml (2 tsp) cornflour |
| 30 ml (2 tbsp) dry sherry |
| 15 ml (1 tbsp) soy sauce |
| 15 ml (1 tbsp) hoisin sauce (see box) |
| 5 ml (1 tsp) soft brown sugar |
| 150 ml ($\frac{1}{4}$ pint) water |
| 75 g (3 oz) unsalted cashew nuts |
| salt and freshly ground pepper |

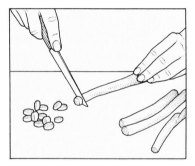

1 Prepare the vegetables. Trim the spring onions and slice them into thin rings. Trim the celery and slice finely.

2 Halve the green pepper, remove the core and seeds and slice the flesh into thin strips. Divide the cauliflower florets into tiny sprigs.

3 Peel the carrots, then grate into thin slivers using the coarse side of a conical or box grater or cut into matchsticks. Wipe the mushrooms and slice them finely.

4 Skin the chicken and cut into bite-sized strips about 4 cm (1$\frac{1}{2}$ inches) long with a sharp knife.

5 Heat the oil in a wok or deep frying pan, add the prepared vegetables and stir-fry over brisk heat for 3 minutes. Remove with a slotted spoon and set aside.

6 In a jug, mix the cornflour to a paste with the sherry, soy sauce and hoisin sauce, then add the sugar and water.

7 Add the chicken strips to the pan and stir-fry over moderate heat until lightly coloured on all sides. Pour the cornflour mixture into the pan and bring to the boil, stirring constantly until thickened.

8 Return the vegetables to the pan. Add the cashew nuts and seasoning to taste, and stir-fry for a few minutes more. Serve immediately.

STIR-FRIED CHICKEN WITH VEGETABLES AND CASHEW NUTS

The hoisin sauce used in this Chinese-style recipe is just one of the many bottled and canned sauces which are used frequently in Chinese cookery. Look for them in oriental specialist shops and some large supermarkets — they will give an 'authentic' touch to your oriental dishes.

Chinese cooks use commercial sauces all the time. Hoisin sauce is made from soya bean flour, sugar, spices and food colouring; it is thick and pungent, a reddish-brown in colour. Add it to any stir-fried dish for extra body and flavour, and use it in sweet and sour dishes.

GINGERED CHICKEN

| 1.00 | 🍴 | £ | 361 cals |

Serves 4

| 1.4-kg (3-lb) oven-ready chicken |
| 15 ml (1 tbsp) plain flour |
| 15 ml (1 tbsp) ground ginger |
| 60 ml (4 tbsp) vegetable oil |
| 1 onion, skinned and sliced |
| 283-g (10-oz) can bamboo shoots |
| 1 red pepper, halved, seeded and sliced |
| 150 ml ($\frac{1}{4}$ pint) chicken stock |
| 45 ml (3 tbsp) soy sauce |
| 45 ml (3 tbsp) medium dry sherry |
| salt and freshly ground pepper |
| 100 g (4 oz) mushrooms, sliced |

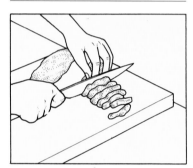

1 Cut all the flesh off the chicken and slice into chunky 'fingers', discarding the skin.

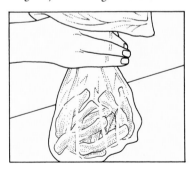

2 Mix the flour and ginger together in a polythene bag and toss the chicken in it to coat.

3 Heat the oil in a very large sauté or deep frying pan and fry the chicken and sliced onion together for 10–15 minutes until they are both golden.

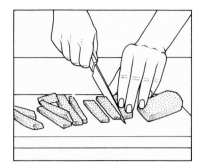

4 Cut up the canned bamboo shoots into 1-cm ($\frac{1}{2}$-inch) strips; add to the pan, together with the sliced pepper. Then stir in stock, soy sauce, sherry and seasoning. Bring to boil, cover, simmer 15 minutes.

5 Add the sliced mushrooms, cover again with lid and cook for a further 5–10 minutes, or until the chicken is tender.

BAMBOO SHOOTS

These are used extensively in oriental cooking, although the Chinese and Japanese use fresh shoots rather than the canned ones specified in this recipe. If fresh bamboo shoots are not obtainable, buy canned ones which are available at oriental specialist stores, large supermarkets and delicatessens. These make a very convenient substitute—they are pre-cooked, so all they need is draining and heating through.

The flavour of bamboo shoots is very difficult to describe. Some say they taste like mild asparagus, although asparagus afficionadoes would probably disagree! Look for those canned in water rather than those canned in vinegar—they will have a milder flavour.

BANG BANG CHICKEN

| 2.00* | ⎕ | 252–378 cals |

* plus cooling and overnight marinating

Serves 4–6

15 ml (1 tbsp) finely chopped fresh root ginger

1.4 kg (3 lb) chicken

salt and freshly ground pepper

60 ml (4 tbsp) soy sauce

3 carrots, peeled and very thinly sliced

75 g (3 oz) beansprouts

60 ml (4 tbsp) vegetable oil

30 ml (2 tbsp) sesame oil

30 ml (2 tbsp) sesame seeds

10 ml (2 tsp) crushed dried red chillies

5 ml (1 tsp) soft brown sugar

45 ml (3 tbsp) dry sherry

lettuce, to serve

spring onion tassels, to garnish

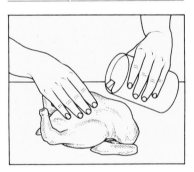

1 Put the ginger inside the cavity of the chicken, then rub the outside of the bird with salt and pepper. Place the bird in a large saucepan and sprinkle over half of the soy sauce. Leave to stand for 30 minutes.

2 Pour enough water into the pan to just cover the chicken. Bring to the boil, then lower the heat, cover and simmer for about 1 hour until the chicken is tender. Leave to cool in the cooking liquid, then remove.

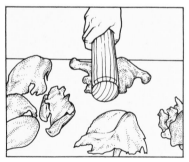

3 Separate the legs and wings from the carcass, then cut the carcass into four. Bang the pieces several times with a rolling pin to loosen the meat from the bones.

4 Cut the meat into neat slices (not too small) or strips. Discard the bones and skin. Combine with carrots and beansprouts.

5 Heat the oils in a heavy-based pan, add the sesame seeds and chillies and fry over brisk heat for a few minutes, stirring until lightly coloured. Remove from the heat and stir in the remaining soy sauce with the sugar and sherry.

6 Pour over the chicken and vegetables, cover and marinate in the refrigerator overnight.

7 To serve, put the chicken and vegetables into a shallow serving dish, lined with lettuce leaves. Pour over any remaining marinade and garnish with spring onion tassels. Serve cold.

STIR-FRIED CHICKEN WITH WALNUTS

0.20*	358 cals

* plus at least 1 hour marinating

Serves 4

4 boneless chicken breasts, skinned and cut into thin strips

5-cm (2-inch) piece of fresh root ginger, peeled and thinly sliced

60 ml (4 tbsp) soy sauce

60 ml (4 tbsp) dry sherry

5 ml (1 tsp) five-spice powder

45 ml (3 tbsp) sesame or vegetable oil

30 ml (2 tbsp) cornflour

150 ml ($\frac{1}{4}$ pint) chicken stock

salt and freshly ground pepper

75 g (3 oz) walnut pieces

$\frac{1}{4}$ cucumber, cut into chunks

spring onion tassels, to garnish

1 Put the chicken in a bowl with the ginger, soy sauce, sherry and five-spice powder. Stir well to mix, then cover and marinate for at least 1 hour.

2 Remove the chicken and ginger from the marinade with a slotted spoon. Reserve marinade.

3 Heat 30 ml (2 tbsp) of the oil in a wok or large heavy-based frying pan. Add the chicken and stir-fry over brisk heat for 5 minutes until well browned.

4 Mix the marinade with the cornflour then stir in the stock. Pour into the pan and bring to the boil, then add salt and pepper to taste and stir-fry for a further 5 minutes or until the chicken strips are tender.

5 Heat the remaining oil in a separate small pan, add the walnuts and cucumber and stir-fry briefly to heat through.

6 Transfer the chicken mixture to a warmed serving dish and top with the walnuts and cucumber. Garnish with spring onion tassels and serve.

PEKING DUCK WITH PANCAKES

2.00* ☐ ☐ £ £ 1094 cals

* plus overnight hanging

Serves 2

2 kg (4 lb) oven-ready duckling, cleaned

60 ml (4 tbsp) dark soft brown sugar

30 ml (2 tbsp) soy sauce

100 g (4 oz) plain flour

salt

a little vegetable oil, for brushing

hoisin sauce, cucumber and spring onions, to serve

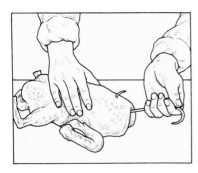

1 Wash the duckling well inside and out, then pat thoroughly dry with absorbent kitchen paper. Insert a meat hook in the neck.

2 Put the sugar and soy sauce in a saucepan with 300 ml ($\frac{1}{2}$ pint) water. Heat gently until the sugar has dissolved, then boil for 5 minutes. Remove from the heat.

3 Brush the sugar syrup over the skin of the duckling several times. Hang the bird up in a cool, airy place with a pan underneath to catch any drips. Leave overnight.

4 The next day, put the duckling on a rack in a roasting tin and pour water underneath to cover the bottom of the tin. Roast the duckling in the oven at 200°C (400°F) mark 6 for 1$\frac{1}{2}$ hours.

5 Meanwhile, make the pancakes. Mix the flour and a pinch of salt in a bowl, then pour in 120 ml (4 fl oz) boiling water. Stir vigorously to a stiff dough with chopsticks or a wooden spoon.

6 Divide the dough into 6 equal pieces. Roll each piece into a ball, then flatten with the heel of your hand and roll out to a 6 cm (2$\frac{1}{2}$ inch) round.

7 Brush 3 of the rounds with a little oil, then sandwich the remaining rounds on top. Roll out each 'sandwich' on a lightly floured surface until 15 cm (6 inches) in diameter. Cover with a damp, clean tea-towel.

8 When the duckling is cooked, transfer to a warmed serving platter and keep hot in the oven turned to its lowest setting.

9 Heat a small, heavy-based frying pan until very hot. Add 1 pancake 'sandwich' and cook until air bubbles appear on the surface. Turn over and repeat cooking on the other side.

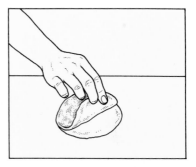

10 Remove the pancakes from the pan and carefully peel them apart. Fold in half, place on a plate and cover with a damp, clean tea-towel. Repeat until all the pancakes are cooked.

11 Serve the duckling and pancakes hot, with hoisin sauce, spring onions and cucumber handed separately.

PEKING DUCK WITH PANCAKES

Peking duck is the perfect main course for an informal Chinese-style supper party. Each person helps themselves to a pancake, spreads a little hoisin sauce over, then tops it with a few slices of duck meat and crispy skin and a few pieces of spring onion and cucumber. The pancake is then rolled up neatly around the filling and eaten with the fingers.

Hoisin sauce, sometimes also called barbecue sauce, is available in bottles from oriental specialist shops and some large supermarkets; once opened, store it in the refrigerator.

SWEET AND SOUR DUCK JOINTS

1.00	458 cals

Serves 4

4 duck portions
salt and freshly ground pepper
60 ml (4 tbsp) soy sauce
45 ml (3 tbsp) soft brown sugar
45 ml (3 tbsp) honey
45 ml (3 tbsp) wine or cider vinegar
30 ml (2 tbsp) dry sherry
juice of 1 orange
150 ml ($\frac{1}{4}$ pint) water
2.5 ml ($\frac{1}{2}$ tsp) ground ginger
few orange slices and watercress
   sprigs, to garnish

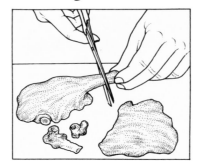

4 Trim the duck joints neatly by cutting off any knuckles or wing joints. Arrange the duck on a warmed serving platter and coat with some of the sauce. Garnish with orange and watercress. Hand remaining sauce separately.

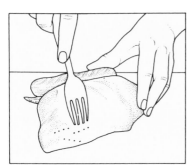

1 Prick the duck portions all over with a fork, then sprinkle the skin liberally with salt and freshly ground pepper.

2 Place on a rack in a roasting tin and roast in the oven at 190°C (375°F) mark 5 for 45–60 minutes until the skin is crisp and the juices run clear when the thickest part of each joint is pierced with a skewer.

3 Meanwhile, make the sauce. Mix together all the remaining ingredients in a saucepan and bring to the boil. Simmer, stirring constantly, for about 5 minutes to allow the flavours to blend and the sauce to thicken slightly. Add salt and pepper to taste.

DUCK WITH MANGO

| 0.35 | £ £ | 683 cals |

Serves 4

1 ripe, but still firm mango

4 duck portions, about 275 g (10 oz) each

60 ml (4 tbsp) peanut oil

2.5 ml ($\frac{1}{2}$ tsp) ground allspice

45 ml (3 tbsp) plum jam

20 ml (4 tsp) wine vinegar

salt and freshly ground pepper

3 Heat the oil in a wok or large frying pan until hot and smoking. Add the duck pieces and allspice. Brown well on all sides.

4 Stir in the plum jam and wine vinegar. Cook for a further 2–3 minutes, stirring constantly, until well glazed. Stir in the mango slices with seasoning to taste. Heat through, then turn into a warmed serving dish and serve immediately.

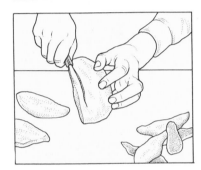

1 Skin and thickly slice the mango on either side of the large central stone.

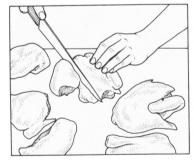

2 Remove any excess fat from the duck portions. Divide each portion into three and place in a saucepan. Cover with cold water and bring to the boil. Lower the heat and simmer gently for 15–20 minutes. Drain well and pat dry with absorbent kitchen paper. Trim bones.

DEVILLED DUCKLING SALAD

| 2.15* | £ £ | 390 cals |

* plus 2–3 hours chilling

Serves 6

two 1.4-kg (3-lb) oven-ready
    ducklings

salt

142 ml (5 fl oz) soured cream

90 ml (6 tbsp) mayonnaise

15 ml (1 tbsp) clear honey

15 ml (1 tbsp) mild curry paste

salt and freshly ground pepper

50 g (2 oz) cashew nuts

350 g (12 oz) fresh apricots, stoned
    and thickly sliced

endive leaves, to serve

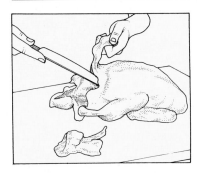

1 Cut away any surplus fat from the ducklings, then wipe them with a damp cloth. Pat dry.

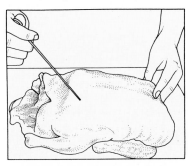

2 Prick the birds all over with a sharp fork or skewer and sprinkle generously with salt. Place the ducklings, breast-side down, side by side on a wire rack or trivet in a large roasting tin.

3 Roast in the oven at 180°C (350°F) mark 4 for about 1¾ hours, or until the birds are really tender, basting occasionally. Halfway through the cooking time, turn the birds over so they are standing breast-side up.

4 Meanwhile, prepare the dressing. In a large bowl, mix together the soured cream, mayonnaise, honey and curry paste. Season and stir in the cashew nuts and apricots.

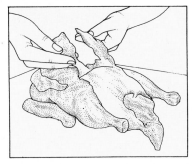

5 While the ducklings are still warm, strip off the crisp breast skin and reserve. Remove the meat from the bones.

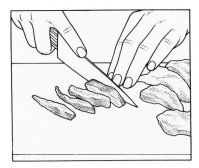

6 Coarsely shred the meat, discarding all the remaining skin, fat and bones. Fold the shredded duckling meat into the dressing, cover and chill well for 2–3 hours in the refrigerator.

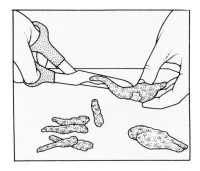

7 Using a pair of kitchen scissors, cut the reserved duckling skin into strips and quickly crisp it further under a hot grill.

8 To serve, spoon the duckling salad down the centre of a large flat platter, then arrange the crisp duck skin over the top. Serve on a bed of endive leaves.

DUCKLINGS

The Chinese were the first to eat ducklings – as long ago as 168 BC! The nobles of the Han dynasty used to breed domestic white ducks for the table – especially for banquets and royal feasts, and they also enjoyed wild duck in stews for more humble occasions. In those days duck meat was served completely unseasoned, and was recommended as a sacrificial offering to appease the gods. Duck soup was also recommended as a remedy for estranged husband and wives – a drop of duck soup was supposed to bring the couple back together again!

    Henry the Eighth had a passion for duck, and was said to retire to bed at night on a supper of roast duckling – not the ideal food for a good night's sleep, but certainly rich enough to satisfy his notoriously large appetite!

SEAFOOD STIR FRY

| 0.25 | £ | 288 cals |

Serves 4

2 celery sticks, washed and
  trimmed

1 medium carrot, peeled

350 g (12 oz) coley, haddock or cod
  fillet, skinned

350 g (12 oz) Iceberg or Cos lettuce

about 45 ml (3 tbsp) peanut oil

1 garlic clove, skinned and crushed

100 g (4 oz) peeled prawns

425 g (15 oz) can whole baby
  sweetcorn, drained

5 ml (1 tsp) anchovy essence

salt and freshly ground pepper

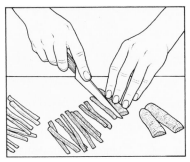

1 Slice the celery and carrot into
thin matchsticks, 5 cm (2 inch)
long. Cut the fish into 2.5 cm
(1 inch) chunks.

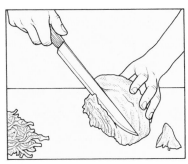

2 Shred the lettuce finely with a
sharp knife, discarding the
core and any thick stalks.

3 Heat 15 ml (1 tbsp) of the oil
in a wok or large frying pan
until smoking. Add the lettuce and
fry for about 30 seconds until
lightly cooked. Transfer to a
serving dish with a slotted spoon
and keep warm in a low oven.

4 Heat another 30 ml (2 tbsp) of
oil in the pan until smoking.
Add the celery, carrot, white fish
and garlic and stir-fry over high
heat for 2–3 minutes, adding
more oil if necessary.

5 Lower the heat, add the
prawns, baby sweetcorn and
anchovy essence. Toss well
together for 2–3 minutes to heat
through and coat all the ingredients in the sauce (the fish will
flake apart).

6 Add seasoning to taste, spoon
on top of the lettuce and serve
immediately.

SEAFOOD STIR FRY

It may seem unusual to stir fry
lettuce, which is usually only
served as a raw salad vegetable,
but it is a method often used in
Chinese cookery. As long as you
use the crisp varieties suggested
here—Iceberg or Cos—you will
find it gives a fresh, crunchy
texture to the dish which
contrasts well with the softness
of the fish. Avoid using round or
cabbage lettuces, which would
become limp on cooking, and
make sure to time the cooking
accurately.

CHINESE VEGETABLE STIR-FRY

| 0.30 | £ | 267 cals |

Serves 4

350 g (12 oz) mangetout

2 large red peppers

1 bunch of spring onions

225 g (8 oz) can water chestnuts

5 cm (2 inch) piece of fresh root
  ginger

1–2 garlic cloves

30 ml (2 tbsp) vegetable oil

15 ml (1 tbsp) sesame oil (optional)

30 ml (2 tbsp) dry sherry

30 ml (2 tbsp) soy sauce

10 ml (2 tsp) honey or soft brown
  sugar

10 ml (2 tsp) tomato purée

salt and freshly ground pepper

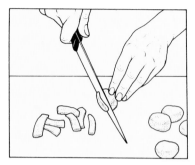

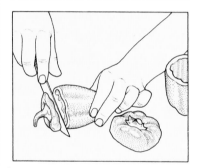

1 First prepare the vegetables. Top and tail the mangetout. Cut the tops off the peppers, remove the cores and seeds and wash thoroughly inside and out.

2 Pat the peppers dry with absorbent kitchen paper, then shred the flesh finely. Trim and shred the spring onions.

3 Drain the water chestnuts, rinse under cold running water, then shred finely.

4 Peel the root ginger, then cut the flesh into matchstick lengths. Skin and crush the garlic.

5 Heat the oils in a wok or deep, heavy-based frying pan. Add the spring onions, ginger and garlic and stir fry for 2–3 minutes. Add the remaining prepared vegetables and stir fry to mix them together.

6 In a bowl or jug, mix together the remaining ingredients, with salt and pepper to taste. Pour over the vegetables, moisten with about 60 ml (4 tbsp) water and mix well. Cook for about 5 minutes, stirring constantly, until the mangetout and red peppers are tender but still crunchy. Transfer to a warmed serving bowl and serve immediately.

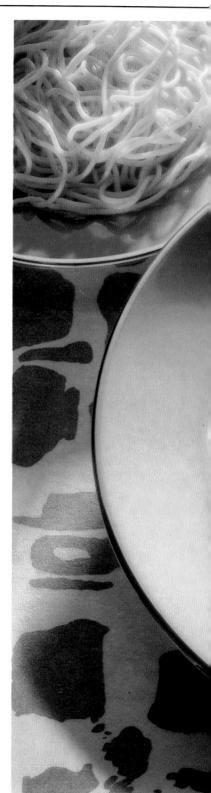

CHINESE VEGETABLE STIR-FRY

Fresh water chestnuts are sometimes available in oriental specialist shops, but canned water chestnuts can be bought from most large supermarkets and delicatessens. Water chestnuts are not actually chestnuts, but the sweet root-bulb of an Asian marsh plant. The canned variety are ready peeled and have a good crunchy texture. They are bland tasting, so need to be combined with strong-tasting foods.

TOFU AND VEGETABLES IN SPICY COCONUT SAUCE

| 1.00 | 🍲 | £ | 271 cals |

Serves 4

75 g (3 oz) creamed coconut

225 g (8 oz) firm or pressed tofu (beancurd)

vegetable oil, for deep frying, plus 45 ml (3 tbsp)

6 spring onions, trimmed and finely chopped

2.5 cm (1 inch) piece of fresh root ginger, peeled and finely chopped

1 garlic clove, skinned and crushed

2.5 ml ($\frac{1}{2}$ tsp) turmeric

2.5 ml ($\frac{1}{2}$ tsp) chilli powder

30 ml (2 tbsp) soy sauce

4 medium carrots, peeled and cut into matchstick strips

225 g (8 oz) cauliflower florets, separated into small sprigs

175 g (6 oz) French beans, topped and tailed

175 g (6 oz) beansprouts

salt and freshly ground pepper

1 First make the coconut milk. Cut the creamed coconut into small pieces and place in a measuring jug. Pour in boiling water up to the 900 ml (1$\frac{1}{2}$ pint) mark. Stir until dissolved, then strain through a muslin-lined sieve. Set aside.

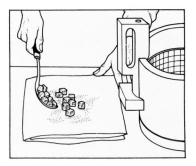

2 Drain the tofu and cut into cubes. Pat thoroughly dry with absorbent kitchen paper. Heat the oil to 190°C (375°F) in a wok or deep-fat frier. Deep-fry the cubes of tofu in the hot oil until golden brown on all sides, turning them frequently with a slotted spoon. Remove and drain on absorbent kitchen paper.

3 Heat the 45 ml (3 tbsp) oil in a heavy-based saucepan or flameproof casserole. Add the spring onions, ginger and garlic and fry gently for about 5 minutes until softened.

4 Add the turmeric and chilli powder and stir fry for 1–2 minutes, then add the coconut milk and soy sauce and bring to the boil, stirring all the time. Add carrots and cauliflower. Simmer, uncovered, for 10 minutes.

5 Add the French beans and simmer for a further 5 minutes, then add the tofu and beansprouts and heat through. Add salt and pepper to taste, then turn into a warmed serving dish. Serve immediately.

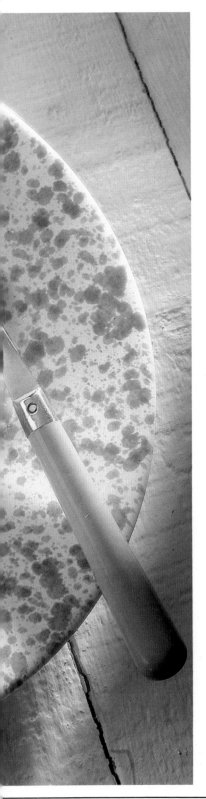

CHINESE FRIED RICE

$\boxed{0.20*}$ ⊟ £ $\boxed{475 \text{ cals}}$

* plus 50 minutes soaking, and 2–3 hours or overnight chilling

Serves 4

350 g (12 oz) long grain rice

3 Chinese dried mushrooms, or 100 g (4 oz) button mushrooms, sliced

4 spring onions

30 ml (2 tbsp) vegetable oil

100 g (4 oz) beansprouts

100 g (4 oz) canned bamboo shoot, drained and cut into 2.5 cm (1 inch) matchsticks

100 g (4 oz) frozen peas

30 ml (2 tbsp) soy sauce

3 eggs, beaten

1 Put the rice in a sieve and wash thoroughly under cold running water until the water runs clear. Transfer the rice to a bowl, cover with cold water and leave to soak for 30 minutes.

2 Drain the rice and put in a medium saucepan. Cover with enough cold water to come 2.5 cm (1 inch) above the rice. Bring to the boil, cover tightly and simmer the rice very gently for 20 minutes. Do not stir.

3 Remove the pan from the heat, leave to cool for 20 minutes, then cover with cling film and chill in the refrigerator for 2–3 hours or overnight.

4 When ready to fry the rice, put the dried mushrooms in a bowl, cover with boiling water and leave to soak for about 20 minutes or until soft.

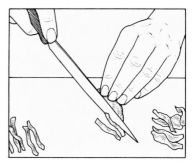

5 Squeeze out any excess moisture from the mushrooms, then cut into thin slivers. Cut the spring onions diagonally into 2.5 cm (1 inch) lengths.

6 Heat the oil in a wok or deep, heavy-based frying pan over high heat. Add all the vegetables and stir fry for 2–3 minutes. Add the soy sauce and cook, briefly, stirring.

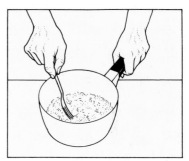

7 Fork up the rice, add to the pan and stir fry for 2 minutes. Pour in the beaten eggs and continue to stir fry for 2–3 minutes, or until the egg has scrambled and the rice is heated through. Serve immediately.

ORIENTAL RICE RING

1.00*	565 cals

* plus at least 4 hours or overnight chilling

Serves 4

225 g (8 oz) brown rice

salt and freshly ground pepper

40 g (1½ oz) creamed coconut

105 ml (7 tbsp) vegetable oil

15 ml (1 tbsp) soy sauce

15 ml (1 tbsp) wine vinegar

5 ml (1 tsp) clear honey

2 carrots

1 red pepper

75 g (3 oz) beansprouts

25 g (1 oz) unsalted peanuts, chopped

15 ml (1 tbsp) lemon juice

1 Cook the brown rice in plenty of boiling salted water until tender; about 30 minutes or according to packet instructions.

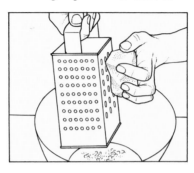

2 Meanwhile, grate the creamed coconut into a bowl. Add 60 ml (4 tbsp) of the oil, the soy sauce, vinegar and honey and beat well to mix.

3 Drain the rice well and tip into the bowl of dressing. Stir quickly to mix, add seasoning to taste, then spoon into a lightly oiled 900 ml (1½ pint) ring mould. Press down well, cover and chill in the refrigerator for at least 4 hours, or overnight if more convenient.

4 Prepare the vegetables. Scrape the carrots, then grate them finely. Cut the red pepper in half, remove the core and seeds, then cut the flesh into thin strips.

5 Combine the carrots, red pepper, beansprouts and peanuts with the remaining oil and the lemon juice. Add seasoning to taste.

6 Turn the rice ring out on to a flat serving plate. Pile the salad in the centre just before serving.

RICE SALAD

0.40*	f	577 cals

* plus 1 hour cooling

Serves 4

275 g (10 oz) long grain brown rice

salt and freshly ground pepper

1 head of fennel

1 red pepper

175 g (6 oz) beansprouts

75 g (3 oz) cashew nuts

90 ml (6 tbsp) corn or vegetable oil

finely grated rind and juice of
   1 large orange

few orange segments, to garnish

1 Cook the brown rice in plenty of boiling salted water for 30 minutes (or according to packet instructions), until tender but firm to the bite.

2 Meanwhile, prepare the remaining ingredients. Trim the fennel, reserving a few feathery tops for the garnish. Cut the top off the red pepper and remove the core and seeds. Wash the pepper and pat dry with absorbent kitchen paper.

3 Chop the fennel and red pepper finely. Wash the beansprouts and drain well. Chop the cashew nuts roughly.

4 In a jug, whisk the oil, orange rind and juice together, with salt and pepper to taste.

5 Drain the rice thoroughly, then turn into a bowl. Add the dressing while the rice is still hot and toss well to combine. Leave to stand for about 1 hour, or until the rice is cold.

6 Add the prepared vegetables and nuts to the rice and toss well to mix. Taste and adjust seasoning. Turn the salad into a serving bowl and garnish with the reserved fennel tops and the orange segments. Serve at room temperature.

CHEESE, BEANSPROUT AND PINEAPPLE SALAD

| 0.15 | £ | 211 cals |

Serves 4

275 g (10 oz) beansprouts
225 g (8 oz) carrots, peeled
225 g (8 oz) Edam cheese
227 g (8 oz) can pineapple slices in
 natural juice
10 ml (2 tsp) wine vinegar
salt and freshly ground pepper

1 Wash the beansprouts. Drain well. Cut the carrots into 2.5 cm (1 inch) matchstick thin strips. Coarsely grate the cheese.

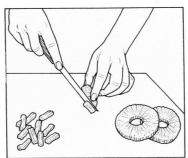

2 Drain the pineapple, reserving the juice. Cut the pineapple into thin strips.

3 In a large bowl, mix together the beansprouts, carrot, cheese and pineapple. Cover and chill in the refrigerator until required.

4 Make the dressing. Whisk the pineapple juice and vinegar together with seasoning to taste.

5 Just before serving, pour the dressing over the salad and toss well to mix. Serve at room temperature.

CHEESE, BEANSPROUT AND PINEAPPLE SALAD

Instead of the Edam cheese used here, use the same amount of tofu, available from the chilling cabinets in health food shops and some large supermarkets. Tofu is a curd made from soya beans — the beans are ground into an emulsion, then curdled with powdered gypsum (rather like rennet curdling milk). The Chinese have used tofu in their cooking for over 2000 years, and it is still eaten today all over China, Japan and East Asia for its health-giving properties. Weight for weight, tofu provides more first-class protein than steak, and for this reason it is extremely popular with vegetarians.

FRESH PINEAPPLE COMPOTE

0.50*	🍳	£ £	114 cals

* plus overnight chilling

Serves 8

2 small ripe pineapples

60 ml (4 tbsp) orange-flavoured liqueur

567 g (1 lb 4 oz) can lychees in syrup

shelled pistachio nuts, to decorate

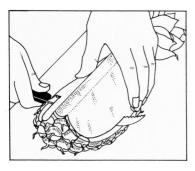

1 Cut each pineapple lengthways into quarters, slicing through the 'crown' at the top. Cut out the hard central cores and discard.

2 Using a serrated knife, carefully cut all around the edge of each pineapple 'boat' between the flesh and the skin.

3 Carefully work the knife underneath the pineapple flesh, to release it completely from the skin. Cut the flesh into bite-sized cubes. Wrap the pineapple shells in cling film and set aside.

4 Put the pineapple cubes in a bowl and sprinkle over the liqueur. Drain the lychees, pouring the syrup into a saucepan. Add three-quarters of the lychees to the pineapple.

5 Boil the lychee syrup until reduced by half, then leave to cool. Add to the pineapple and lychees and fold gently to mix. Cover the bowl with cling film and chill overnight, with the pineapple shells and reserved lychees.

6 Cut the reserved lychees into flower shapes. Divide the pineapple and lychees equally between the 8 shells and pour over the syrup. Decorate with the lychee 'flowers' and pistachios. Serve chilled.

FRESH PINEAPPLE COMPOTE

Canned lychees are available at most good supermarkets. They have a deliciously sweet flavour and unusual texture, and can be used in fruit salads of all kinds to add a touch of exotic interest. Lychees (also called lichees and litchis) are native to China, but they also grow in India and South Africa. The fresh fruit are available at some specialist markets and greengrocers in late summer, but they are not easy to recognise if you are only familiar with the canned fruit. The skin of fresh lychees is rough and brittle, almost like a bark.

MANDARIN AND LYCHEE MOUSSE

| 0.45* | £ | ✳ | 292 cals |

* plus 30 minutes cooling and at least
2 hours setting

Serves 6

3 eggs, separated

2 egg yolks

75 g (3 oz) caster sugar

**298-g (10½-oz) can mandarin
  oranges in natural juice**

310-g (11-oz) can lychees in syrup

15 ml (3 tsp) gelatine

150 ml (5 fl oz) double cream

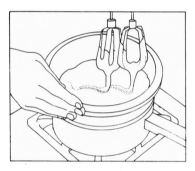

1 Put the 5 egg yolks and sugar
in a large heatproof bowl and
stand over a saucepan of gently
simmering water. Whisk until the
mixture is thick and holds a
ribbon trail, then remove the bowl
from the pan. Leave for 30
minutes, whisking occasionally.

2 Reserve 60 ml (4 tbsp) of the
mandarin juice. Purée half the
oranges and the remaining juice in
a blender or food processor with
the lychees and half the syrup.

3 Put the reserved mandarin
syrup in a heatproof bowl and
sprinkle in the gelatine. Stand the
bowl over a saucepan of hot water
and heat gently until dissolved.
Remove the bowl from the pan
and leave to cool slightly.

4 Stir the mandarin purée into
the cooled egg yolk mixture,
then stir in the gelatine liquid
until evenly mixed.

5 Whip the cream until standing
in soft peaks. Whisk the egg
whites until stiff. Fold first the
cream and then the egg whites into
the mousse until evenly blended.
Turn into a glass serving bowl and
chill for at least 2 hours until set.

6 When the mousse is set serve
decorated with the reserved
mandarin oranges and extra
whipped cream, if liked.

APPLE AND BANANA FRITTERS

| 1.00 | 🍴 | £ | 218–328 cals |

Serves 4–6

100 g (4 oz) plain flour
pinch of salt
90 ml (6 tbsp) lukewarm water
20 ml (4 tsp) vegetable oil
2 egg whites
1 large cooking apple
2 bananas
juice of ½ a lemon
vegetable oil, for deep frying
caster sugar, to serve

1 Place the flour and salt into a bowl. Make a well in the centre. Add the water and oil and beat to form a smooth batter.

2 Beat the egg whites in a clean dry bowl until they are stiff; then set aside.

3 Peel, quarter and core the apple. Peel the bananas. Slice the fruit thickly and sprinkle at once with the lemon juice to prevent discoloration.

4 Fold the beaten egg whites into the batter, then immediately dip in the slices of fruit.

5 Deep-fry the fritters a few at a time in hot oil until puffed and light golden. Remove with a slotted spoon and pile on to a serving dish lined with absorbent kitchen paper. Serve immediately, sprinkled with caster sugar.

MELON AND GINGER SORBET

0.30* £ ✳ 80 cals

* plus 6 hours freezing and 30 minutes softening

Serves 6

75 g (3 oz) sugar

1 medium honeydew melon

45 ml (3 tbsp) lemon juice

1 piece preserved stem ginger, finely chopped

few drops green food colouring (optional)

2 egg whites

1 Dissolve the sugar slowly in 300 ml (½ pint) water. Bring to the boil, bubble for 2 minutes, then transfer to a bowl and leave the sugar syrup to cool.

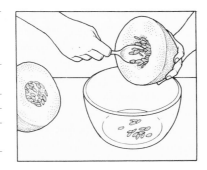

2 Halve the melon, remove the seeds and scoop out the flesh. Purée the flesh in a blender or a food processor until smooth. Stir into the cool syrup with the lemon juice. Then add the chopped stem ginger and a few drops of green food colouring, if wished.

3 Freeze the sorbet in a shallow container for about 3 hours until mushy in texture. Whisk the egg whites until stiff and fold into the sorbet mixture. Return to the freezer for a further 3 hours until the sorbet is firm.

4 To serve, remove from the freezer and place in the refrigerator for about 30 minutes to soften slightly. Serve in individual glasses, with fan wafers if liked.

INDEX

GOOD HOUSEKEEPING

...For the life women <u>REALLY</u> lead

Dear Reader,

We do hope you will enjoy your **Good Housekeeping** cookery book and will go on to collect the other titles available from your **BP Service Station.** Each recipe given has been double tested for success by our highly respected and unique resource, the **Good Housekeeping Institute,** so you can try new dishes with complete confidence.

It is that same confidence and trust that makes millions of women read our **Good Housekeeping** magazine each month. Colourful and glossy, it is always brimming over with new and exciting ideas, plus practical advice on a huge range of topics that affect all our everyday lives. No wonder so many people now subscribe to **Good Housekeeping** each month to ensure they don't miss a single copy.

Uniquely for BP customers we are offering a special introductory rate to all new UK subscribers of only £11.20 — *a saving of £2 on the current rate!* For this amount you will receive a copy of Good Housekeeping by post each month for 12 months.

Credit card holders can order by telephoning 0444 440421 or by post to the address below.

Happy reading!

Brian Braithwaite

Brian Braithwaite
Publishing Director — Good Housekeeping

Subscription enquiries and orders with payment to:
Quadrant Subscription Services, FREEPOST, Haywards Heath, West Sussex RH16 3ZA.
Offer closes 31st August 1989.

IMPORTANT: TO QUALIFY FOR YOUR DISCOUNT QUOTE "SAK" IN ALL COMMUNICATIONS.

Published by Ebury Press
Division of The National Magazine Company Ltd
Colquhoun House
27–37 Broadwick Street
London W1V 1FR

The Good Housekeeping Institute is the food and consumer research centre of
Good Housekeeping magazine.

Printed and bound in Italy by New Interlitho, S.p.a., Milan